Date: 8/17/18

J 796.357 VEN
Ventura, Marne,
STEM in baseball /

STEM IN BASEBALL

SportsZone

An Imprint of Abdo Publishing
abdopublishing.com

BY MARNE VENTURA

ABDOPUBLISHING.COM

Published by Abdo Publishing, a division of ABDO, PO Box 398166, Minneapolis, Minnesota 55439.
Copyright © 2018 by Abdo Consulting Group, Inc. International copyrights reserved in all countries.
No part of this book may be reproduced in any form without written permission from the
publisher. SportsZone™ is a trademark and logo of Abdo Publishing.

Printed in the United States of America, North Mankato, Minnesota
102017
012018

THIS BOOK CONTAINS
RECYCLED MATERIALS

Cover Photo: Chris Carlson/AP Images
Interior Photos: Chris Carlson/AP Images, 1; Chris Williams/Icon Sportswire/AP Images, 4–5,
38–39; Tom DiPace/AP Images, 6; Peter Joneleit/Cal Sport Media/AP Images, 9; Frank Romeo/
Shutterstock Images, 10–11; Bill Bachmann/Science Source, 12–13; Shutterstock Images, 15, 19 (top),
19 (top middle), 19 (bottom middle), 37 (middle), 37 (bottom); Wally Fong/AP Images, 17; Evgeny
Karandaev/Shutterstock Images, 19 (bottom); David Goldman/AP Images, 20–21; Michael Zagaris/
Oakland Athletics/Getty Images Sport/Getty Images, 23; Dan Thornberg/Shutterstock Images, 25
(left); Red Line Editorial, 25 (right), 37 (top); Gregory Bull/AP Images, 26; Marcio Jose Sanchez/AP
Images, 28–29; Universal History Archive/Universal Images Group/Getty Images, 30–31; Orlando/
Three Lions/Getty Images, 33; Ann Heisenfelt/AP Images, 35; Bizuayehu Tesfaye/AP Images, 41;
Dejan Popovic/Shutterstock Images, 44

Editor: Arnold Ringstad
Series Designer: Maggie Villaume
Content Consultant: Ricardo Valerdi, Associate Professor, The University of Arizona
        College of Engineering

PUBLISHER'S CATALOGING-IN-PUBLICATION DATA
Names: Ventura, Marne, author.
Title: STEM in baseball / by Marne Ventura.
Description: Minneapolis, Minnesota : Abdo Publishing, 2018. | Series: STEM in sports | Includes
        online resources and index.
Identifiers: LCCN 2017946886 | ISBN 9781532113475 (lib.bdg.) | ISBN 9781532152351 (ebook)
Subjects: LCSH: Baseball--Juvenile literature. | Sports sciences--Juvenile literature. | Physics--
        Juvenile literature.
Classification: DDC 796.357--dc23
LC record available at https://lccn.loc.gov/2017946886

TABLE OF CONTENTS

Mike Bolsinger prepares to deliver a powerful pitch.

1

STEM IN THE WORLD OF BASEBALL

The young fan leaned forward in his stadium seat. The smell of hot dogs and popcorn filled the warm Florida air. Like many Miami Marlins fans, he wore an orange T-shirt and black baseball cap.

The date was May 12, 2015. Mike Bolsinger was pitching for the Los Angeles Dodgers. It was the first inning, and the Marlins' Giancarlo Stanton was up to bat.

Stanton has gained a reputation as one of today's strongest hitters.

The fan loved baseball statistics. He knew Bolsinger was a skilled pitcher. He also knew Stanton was a slugger. The fan was a pretty good Little League hitter himself. He watched to see Stanton's stance and how he gripped the bat.

Bolsinger wound up and threw a fastball. *Crack!* Stanton's bat met the ball right at the sweet spot. For a split-second, more than 49,000 fans in the stadium were quiet. The ball shot up over left field, past the outfield wall, and out of the ballpark. The crowd went wild. They jumped up and clapped. They whistled. They screamed. The young fan in the orange shirt whooped and hollered. Stanton's home run traveled 478 feet (146 m).

STEM IN ACTION

Baseball games are fun and exciting. They are also great places to watch science, technology, engineering, and math (STEM) in action. More than 170 years ago, the first baseball club in New York, the Knickerbockers, began using formal rules. Since then, baseball has become one of America's favorite sports. Athletes have gotten better at playing and winning by using STEM. Even if they don't know it, STEM fields are a part of every game.

How is science a part of baseball? Throwing a curveball, hitting the sweet spot on a bat, and running the bases are all subject to the laws of physics. Understanding concepts such as motion, gravity, drag, and friction helps baseball players perform their best. Sports medicine has come a long way, too. Years ago, players with serious injuries had to retire. Today, breakthroughs in medicine allow athletes to return to baseball even after severe medical problems. New information about diet and nutrition helps athletes stay healthy.

Technology has advanced dramatically since the mid-1800s. Fans everywhere can watch the game on television or even on their smartphones. Instant replay videos help players improve their game. They also help umpires confirm that they made the right call. Players use apps to track data and monitor information about their physical progress. Uniforms are better because of advances in fabric and materials.

Engineers play a key role in modern baseball, too. They use a scientific design process to create the best

Technology has become an important part of modern baseball.

bats, balls, gloves, helmets, and stadiums. First they identify a problem that needs to be solved. How can wood bats be made so they don't break as easily? Which helmet best protects a player's head? Next they do research. They define the requirements for a good bat or helmet. They brainstorm solutions, try them out, and improve their products.

Math and baseball have been partners since the game began. Every game creates new statistics and averages. Fans and players alike keep track of how many earned runs the pitcher allows over nine innings.

A player's batting average shows how often he gets on base with a hit. Teams have winning percentages and batters have slugging percentages. With the advent of computers and the Internet, everyone can see the numbers from a game as soon as they happen. Team managers now make many of their decisions based on statistics.

STEM plays a role in every area of the game, from the fans in the stands to home plate to the outfield wall.

STEM plays a role in every part of baseball, from how it's played to how it's managed to how it's watched. The game's traditions may be more than 170 years old, but baseball has benefited from advances in these fields. Science, technology, engineering, and math make the modern game of baseball work.

Science is at work when kids play baseball with their friends and when professionals are playing in the major leagues.

2

THE SCIENCE OF BASEBALL

Scientists study the makeup and behavior of the physical and natural world. They do this by observing and experimenting. Athletes and trainers use science to improve performance and win more games. Three areas of science that are especially important in sports are physics, medicine, and nutrition.

THE PHYSICS OF A PITCH

According to the laws of physics, the more force is applied to an object, the faster it will move. An object will keep moving in the same direction and at the same speed until a force slows it down. When a pitcher throws a fastball, the force of his throw puts the ball into motion. Gravity pulls the ball down toward the ground. Air resistance generates drag, which decreases its speed.

When a pitcher puts spin on the ball, it changes the way the air moves around it. To throw a fastball, the pitcher holds the ball loosely. This causes a backspin that creates lift. For a curveball, the pitcher snaps and turns his wrist to give the ball topspin. Curveballs are caused by a phenomenon called the Magnus effect.

MAGNUS EFFECT

How does the Magnus effect cause a pitched baseball to curve? When a ball spins, the air pressure around it changes. On the side of the ball that spins in the direction that the ball is moving, the air pressure is high. On the other side of the ball, the air pressure is low. The high-pressure air pushes toward the low-pressure air. This makes the ball curve instead of moving straight. The effect can also be seen in the flight of tennis balls and soccer balls.

The stitches on a ball help influence its movement through the air.

The ball spins in a downward path as it crosses home plate. Knuckleballs result when the pitcher uses no spin. This can cause the ball to move unpredictably.

THE PHYSICS OF BATTING

The laws of physics also say that for every action there is an equal and opposite reaction. When the bat hits the ball, the ball reacts by moving in a new direction. The force of the collision causes the bat to shake or vibrate.

Most home runs are hit from a spot on the bat about six inches (15 cm) from the top. A collision at this area, known as the sweet spot, causes the least vibration. This means more energy is transferred to the ball, so the ball moves faster off the bat. The batter hears a crack instead of a clunk, and the bat doesn't sting his hands.

GAME-CHANGING MEDICINE AND NUTRITION

Advances in medical technology have enabled baseball players to recover from serious injuries and return to the field. Pitchers are at risk of tearing their ulnar collateral

Today, the type of procedure that John underwent is known as Tommy John surgery.

ligament (UCL), which passes through the elbow joint. Fifty years ago, a UCL tear would have meant the end of a pitcher's career. In 1974, Tommy John, a left-handed pitcher for the Dodgers, suffered this injury. Dr. Frank Jobe, a noted orthopedic surgeon, devised a new kind of surgery. He took a tendon from elsewhere in John's body and used it to replace the damaged ligament. After a year and a half of recovery, John was once again pitching in the major leagues. He played for another 14 years. Today, an average of more than 15 players each year undergo the same surgery.

Modern professional athletes are more health-conscious than ever before. Researchers have confirmed the importance of a diet emphasizing fruits and vegetables, whole grains, lean protein, and plenty of water. The hot dogs, candy, and soda sold at most baseball games are not what top athletes eat on a regular basis. Most teams now hire a nutritionist to help players plan meals for maximum health and performance.

DAIRY FOODS

- Contain calcium, potassium, and Vitamin D
- Important for healthy bones, heart, and blood pressure

VEGETABLES AND FRUITS

- Low in fat and calories, cholesterol-free
- Excellent sources of vitamins, minerals, and fiber
- Important for healthy weight, heart health, and blood pressure

WHOLE GRAINS

- Good source of fiber, B vitamins, and minerals
- Important for heart and blood health
- Help body use energy from food

LEAN PROTEIN FOODS

- Act as building blocks for growth and repair
- Help the body use energy

Smart athletes get fuel for better performance by eating fresh, natural foods. Good nutrition keeps baseball players in top form by supplying the vitamins, minerals, fats, carbohydrates, and protein their bodies need for strength, endurance, and disease prevention. Healthy ballplayers drink plenty of water and get enough sleep each night.

NUTRITION FOR ATHLETES

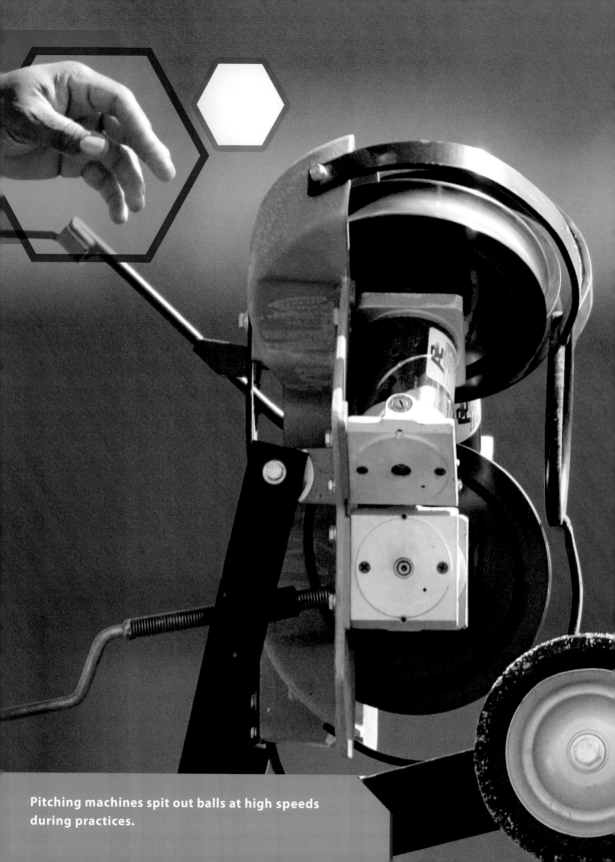

Pitching machines spit out balls at high speeds during practices.

3

HI-TECH BASEBALL

Technology is created when engineers use scientific information for practical purposes, such as building machines and equipment. Pitching machines, digital video, virtual reality, radar tracking, and wearable sensors are all examples of technologies that help baseball players track and improve their performance.

PRACTICE MAKES PERFECT

The first pitching machine, invented in the 1890s, worked like a cannon. When the user pulled a trigger, gunpowder exploded and forced out a ball. In 1952, a safer, better machine was invented. It used a mechanical arm. Combined with a batting cage, it allowed athletes to practice hitting without creating wear and tear on the arm of a human pitcher.

Digital video brought big advancements to baseball. Players in all positions can now see themselves in action. By analyzing their performance with video, they can see where they're succeeding and where they need to improve. Virtual reality (VR) practice lets players wearing headsets pitch and hit in a computer simulation.

VR-ENHANCED BATTING PRACTICE

Virtual reality (VR) is a computer-generated world that users can explore using a headset and headphones. It allows people to experience places that don't physically exist. Three-dimensional video games are examples of virtual reality. For VR batting practice, the athlete wears a headset that enables him to see a pitcher throwing curveballs, fastballs, and knuckleballs. He swings an actual bat at the virtual pitch. He gets feedback from a computer program that helps improve his stance and timing.

Boston Red Sox player Hanley Ramirez studies a tablet before a game in May 2017.

TRACKING TECHNOLOGY

Doppler radar technology can record the speed of a baseball after it's pitched, hit, or thrown. It works by firing radio waves at the ball and analyzing their reflections. Another system tracks the ball and players, creating a three-dimensional video. As the video shows the ball and athlete in action, information about the speed of the ball, the angle and distance of its flight, and the probability of a fielder's catch is also displayed on the screen. Getting instant information is fun for baseball fans. Players use the data to help them measure and improve their performance. Coaches figure out their lineups and decide where to position their players based on these numbers.

HANDHELD AND WEARABLE ELECTRONICS

Major League Baseball (MLB) has approved the use of some devices on the field. Using these new technologies, players can review and improve their

MOVING BALL

KEY

(= waves from radar gun   ) = reflected waves

The term *radar* comes from the phrase *radio detection and ranging*. Radar devices send out radio waves. Those radio waves bounce off an object. Then the reflected radio waves come back to the device. The device senses the reflected waves. Based on how long the reflected waves took to come back, the device can tell how far away the object is.

Doppler radar technology goes one step further. It can find not only an object's location, but also its speed. It takes advantage of a phenomenon called the Doppler effect. The frequency of waves coming from an object increases when the object is moving toward an observer. This can be seen in everyday life, when a police car is using its siren as it drives past a person on the sidewalk. As the police car approaches the person, the speed of the car is combined with the speed of the siren's sound waves. The sound waves bunch up, becoming higher in frequency. The result is a higher-pitched sound.

The Doppler effect can be used to find the speed of a moving baseball. A person points a radar gun at a pitched baseball. The radar gun shoots out radio waves, and they bounce off the baseball. Because the baseball is moving toward the gun, the reflected waves are bunched up, coming back at a higher frequency than the original waves. Sensors and a computer inside the radar gun figure out the difference in frequency. They can use this information to determine the speed of the pitch.

A motion-sensing batting glove is shown off at an electronics trade show.

performance in many ways. One device is a tight-fitting sleeve worn on the player's arm. It records arm angle, pitch count, and other data. Data from the sensors in the sleeve can warn a coach that the pitcher is fatigued, helping prevent injury. Another device is a vest with sensors that's worn under the athlete's uniform. It measures and records heart rate, respiration rate, temperature, and other data. During the game, coaches can monitor a player's health. After the game, players can use the data to help them analyze and improve their performance. A third device is a sensor that goes on the bottom of the bat. It helps players study their swing motions.

Some players, including catchers, wear gear that is
engineered to keep them safe.

4

ENGINEERING BETTER GEAR

An engineer is an expert in designing and building machines, devices, and structures. Engineers find ways to make baseballs, gloves, helmets, and bats work better. Their role in baseball has come a long way. Today's baseball gear is safer than ever before.

BUILDING A BETTER BASEBALL

In the late 1800s, baseballs were made by winding yarn around rubber and sewing on a horsehide cover. By the end of a

game they were lumpy and hard to hit. At the start of

the 1900s, people began using cork in the center of the

balls. Cork is springier than the rubber they were using.

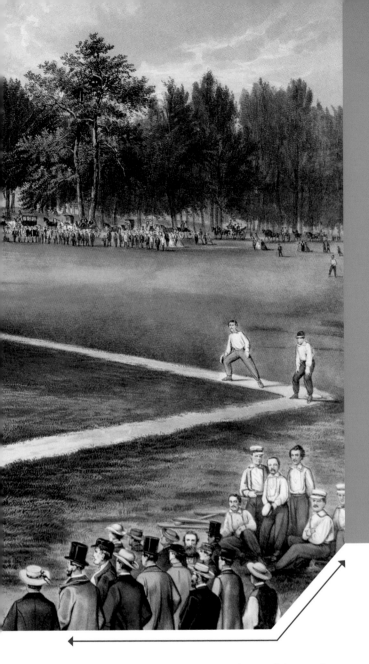

Early in baseball's history, the technology and gear involved were relatively primitive.

Engineers invented machines that wound three layers of wool around the cork. Next a layer of cotton and polyester yarn was added. Finally a white cowhide cover was stitched on with red-waxed thread. This is still the process used today.

Balls used in professional baseball are made to tight guidelines. They must have a circumference between 9 and 9.25 inches (23 and 23.5 cm), a weight between 5 and 5.25 ounces (142 and 149 g), and exactly 108 stitches. When pressed, they must regain their shape to within 0.08 inches (0.2 cm). When thrown at a wood surface, they must bounce back at between 51.4 and 57.8 percent of their starting speed.

SOME THINGS NEVER CHANGE

Despite improvements in baseball engineering in the past 170 years, nobody has been able to make a machine to stitch the cowhide cover onto a professional baseball. A shoe company in Boston, Massachusetts, experimented with a baseball-stitching machine in 1949. Engineers worked for 12 years and spent $343,000, but they were unsuccessful. Today one company in Costa Rica is the only supplier of MLB balls. During a game, the teams will go through five or six dozen balls. Every single one is hand sewn.

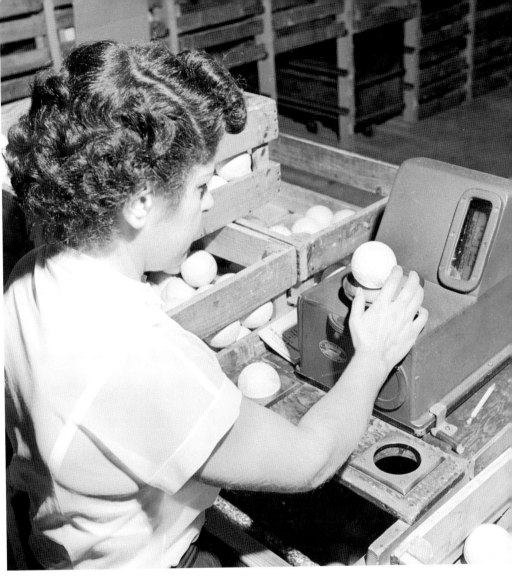

The same basic process has been used to build baseballs for many decades.

PROTECTING HANDS AND HEADS

The first baseball players caught barehanded or wore a thin leather hand cover. By the late 1800s, players were wearing thicker leather gloves. Around 1920, a glove was designed with webbing between the thumb and index finger. The webbing helped the player catch the ball and absorbed the force of the collision. By the 1940s, the fingers of the glove were tied together. Again, this improved catching and helped protect the player's hand. Today's gloves are thicker and more cushioned.

Ray Chapman, a shortstop for the Cleveland Indians, died in 1920 after being hit in the head by a pitched ball. Finally, in 1971, MLB made batting helmets mandatory. Twelve years later, earflaps were required as well. A new helmet introduced in 2013 can protect against the force of a fastball going 100 miles per hour (161 km/h).

THE BEST BATS

As with baseballs, MLB has strict rules about professional bats. A bat has to be a single piece of smooth, round, solid wood. It can't exceed 2.61 inches (6.63 cm) in diameter at the thickest part, or 42 inches (107 cm) in length.

The earliest ballplayers carved their own bats from ash or maple. By the late 1880s, bats were being made by woodworking factories. Since wood bats are expensive and break easily, aluminum bats became popular in college baseball and at lower levels in the 1970s. In addition to being cheaper to make and more durable, the hollow aluminum gave in slightly and didn't compress the ball like wood did. As a result, the ball kept more of its pitched energy. Players were hitting more home runs. Games were longer and scores were higher. Hard hits were injuring more players. The wood bat is still the most popular, and MLB has never allowed aluminum bats in its games.

Two recent developments in baseball bats are the axe bat and the smart bat. The end of an axe bat's handle is slanted like the handle of an axe. It's designed to give the batter better control and faster swing speed. It's also supposed to prevent hand and wrist damage. A smart bat has a sensor on the base that measures swing speed and angles to help the batter improve his technique.

KEY

ALUMINUM BAT (ball leaves bat at 106.5 miles per hour [171.4 km/h])
WOOD BAT (ball leaves bat at 98.6 miles per hour [158.7 km/h])

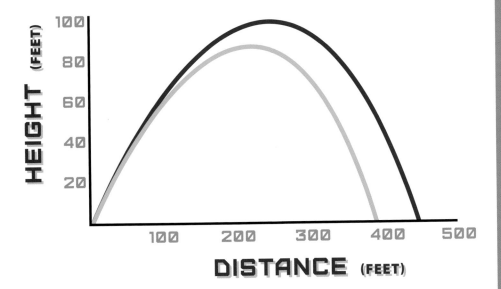

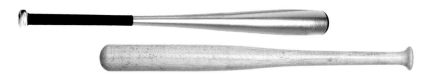

Using an aluminum bat, a player can hit a ball at a faster speed than with a wood bat. The baseball hit with the aluminum bat will travel farther and have a higher arc than the ball hit with a wood bat. The fact that an aluminum bat is hollow, while a wood bat is solid, increases the swing speed. A hollow aluminum bat gives slightly where it meets the ball, and when it springs back it gives the ball an extra push. Why doesn't MLB allow aluminum bats? Most importantly, there would be a danger to players who might get hit with faster line drives. Officials also want the players' performance to be the result of human skill rather than technology.

WOOD VS. ALUMINUM BATS

The amazing catches, hits, and throws that make up a baseball game are translated into many kinds of statistics.

5

CRUNCHING THE NUMBERS

Numbers play a very important role in sports. This is especially true in baseball. Statistics entertain fans and help players, coaches, and owners make big decisions about how to play and win.

FANS DO THE MATH

Baseball lovers have been keeping track of numbers since the game began. In 1859, New York sports reporter Henry Chadwick began publishing a grid of numbers in the newspaper. It reported how many runs were scored, how many hits were made, and other data for both the players and the teams. Chadwick's grid evolved into the modern box score.

Sports fan Bill James began publishing a journal of baseball statistics in the 1970s. He used numbers to understand and predict game outcomes in new ways. Fans and coaches previously judged a player by his batting average. James pointed out that since games are won by scoring runs, better measures of a player's worth are his on-base and slugging percentages. On-base percentage tracks how often a batter gets on base by any means other than by error. Slugging percentage measures how many of his hits go for extra bases— doubles, triples, and home runs.

Today this way of collecting and analyzing data is called sabermetrics, named for the Society for American Baseball Research (SABR), the group that popularized it. Personal computers and the Internet make it easier for

James, who had a major influence on the way baseball statistics are used, was hired as an adviser to the Boston Red Sox in 2003.

baseball fans to get information. In the game of fantasy baseball, fans choose players from various teams who they think will play well. The better the players' stats, the better the fan does. The movie *Moneyball*, starring Brad Pitt, was based on the true story of Billy Beane, the general manager of the Oakland Athletics. While other teams used traditional methods to evaluate players, Beane used a sabermetrics-based approach to find players whose skills were undervalued by the rest of the league. Through this approach, Beane was able to field a competitive team on a much lower budget.

FANTASY BASEBALL

Baseball fans who wish they could own and manage a professional team can live out their dream in fantasy baseball. Fantasy baseball players join a league. This is usually organized online, but sometimes leagues meet in person. At the start of the baseball season, each fantasy player selects real-life MLB players for his or her team. Then, during each actual game, fantasy players score points when the players they chose perform well. The fantasy team with the most points at the end of the season wins.

SAMPLE SIZES AND AVERAGES

Mathematicians can make better predictions when they have more information. If a player gets on base with a hit 6 times out of 20 at-bats, he has a batting average of .300 (6 divided by 20). Knowing the same player got on base 60 times out of 200 at-bats still gives him a batting average of .300, but predicting his chances of getting on base are much stronger. Having this larger sample size results in better statistics.

Statisticians find averages for players and for teams. Averages help fans and managers rank and compare athletes. Averages also help players and fans predict who will win. The earned-run average (ERA) statistic measures how many runs a pitcher allows during nine innings. Slugging percentages tell how many bases are reached by one hit. A winning percentage for a team is found by dividing the number of games won by the total number of games played. Professional baseball players

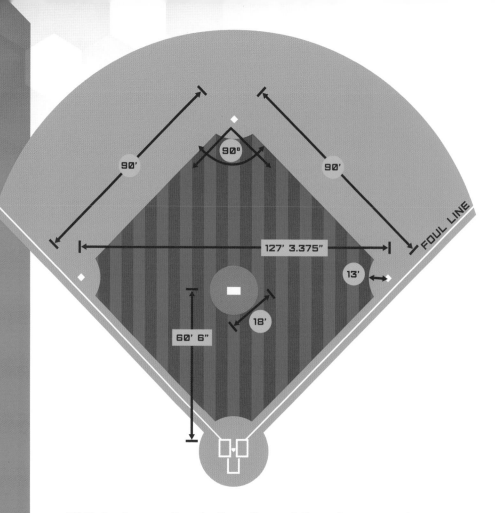

90'

90'

90°

127' 3.375"

13'

18'

60' 6"

FOUL LINE

All Major League Baseball stadiums follow the same rules for the layout of the infield. The diagram shows many of the standard measurements of the infield. However, the size of the outfield varies from stadium to stadium. Why? As baseball parks were built during the past 170 years, they were designed to fit into existing cities and neighborhoods. Their shapes vary depending on their surroundings.

Fenway Park in Boston, Massachusetts, is a good example. A high wall is located behind left field. The wall makes the outfield shorter than other ballparks because it's only 310 feet (94 m) from home plate. The wall has a history of stopping line-drive home runs that would have gone over the outfield wall in other stadiums. It also turns hits that would be routine fly-outs in other parks into home runs.

THE BASEBALL FIELD

use averages to set goals for themselves and to measure their progress.

WHAT'S NEXT?

The world of baseball has come a long way since the 1840s. Science, technology, engineering, and math have played a huge part. What will the future hold for players and fans? MLB team owners and managers are creating new jobs for college graduates with engineering and math degrees. For example, the Houston Astros have a director of decision sciences on staff. He uses data to help drive the team's decision-making process. As the sport of baseball continues to embrace STEM, more careers will open up for scientists, engineers, and mathematicians. Their advances will benefit not only athletes but also the fans who enjoy the game.

GLOSSARY

AVERAGE
The ratio of successful tries to total tries.

INNING
A division of a baseball game, in which each team gets a chance to bat. Nine innings make up a game.

PHENOMENON
An observable fact or event.

PHYSICS
The science of matter, energy, and their interaction.

PROFESSIONAL
Paid to play sports.

RADAR
A device that uses radio waves to locate an object or measure its speed.

SENSOR
A device that collects data from the world around it.

STADIUM
A large building with seating around a sports field.

STATISTICS
A field of mathematics in which numbers and probabilities are studied.

ONLINE RESOURCES

To learn more about STEM in baseball, visit **abdobooklinks.com**. These links are routinely monitored and updated to provide the most current information available.

MORE INFORMATION

BOOKS

Baseball: Then to WOW! New York: Sports Illustrated, 2016.

Jacobs, Greg. *The Everything Kids' Baseball Book: From Baseball's History to Today's Favorite Players – With Lots of Home Run Fun in Between.* Avon, MA: Adams Media, 2014.

Smolka, Bo. *Baseball.* Minneapolis, MN: Abdo Publishing, 2012.

INDEX

ABOUT THE AUTHOR

Marne Ventura is the author of many books for kids, both fiction and nonfiction. She enjoys writing about science, technology, engineering and math, arts and crafts, and the lives of creative people. A former elementary school teacher, Marne holds a master's degree in education from the University of California. She and her husband live on the central coast of California.